Rainforest

Inside Australia's Trop

Meredith Hooper

CAMBRIDGE
UNIVERSITY PRESS

The author would like to thank the Wet Tropics Management Authority,
Queensland, and Stella Martin of the Queensland Department of the Environment.

Contents

Giant birds

Leaves crackle. Something is coming. Suddenly, there is a deep hollow-sounding noise: 'boom, boom, boom, boom'.

A bird appears, walking between the tall tree trunks of the rainforest. It is as tall as an adult human. It has big scaly feet and long sharp claws. The skin of its head and neck is bright blue and red. This bird is a cassowary.

Cassowaries are the largest birds living in the Australian rainforest. They boom when they are angry or when they are about to attack with their powerful feet.

Cassowaries need the rainforest to live in, but the rainforest also needs cassowaries.

Cassowaries eat the fruit from many different rainforest plants. As they walk around the forest, they leave piles of dung. Inside the dung are the seeds of the rainforest fruit. These seeds now have a chance to grow in new places.

Cassowaries spread the seeds of about a hundred different kinds of rainforest plants.

Male cassowaries look after the chicks.

Inside a rainforest

So many plants grow in a rainforest that the leaves form a green roof, called a 'canopy'. Inside the rainforest, trees grow close together, plants grow on plants, and vines push and twist their way up to the canopy. Ferns and palms spread their leaves out. Very little sunlight can get through the canopy down into the forest.

When it rains, the water drips down through the leaves. The air smells damp and warm. You can almost feel the forest growing.

There are more kinds of plants and animals in a rainforest than in any other type of forest. Rainforests are the richest growing places on Earth.

To grow, rainforests need
- ☀ plenty of rain
- ☀ shelter from harsh winds
- ☀ the right kinds of soils
- ☀ the seeds of rainforest plants

Australia's tropical rainforest

Millions of years ago, rainforests covered much of Australia. Now there are only patches of rainforest left.

There are many different kinds of rainforest in Australia. Tropical rainforests grow along the eastern coast of northern Australia, where the mountains are close to the sea and rain falls for much of the year.

These tropical rainforests have been growing for more than 100 million years. They were growing when the dinosaurs were alive. They are some of the oldest rainforests on Earth and contain some of the most ancient types of plants alive today.

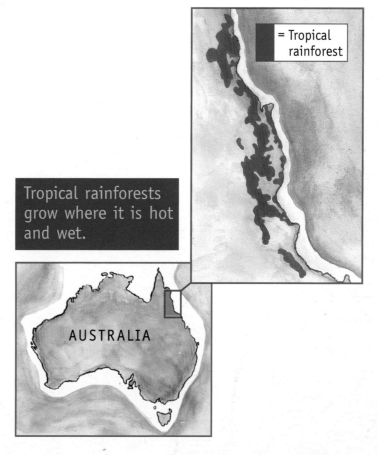

= Tropical rainforest

Tropical rainforests grow where it is hot and wet.

AUSTRALIA

The parts of a tropical rainforest

The rainforest is like a building with a floor, a roof and rooms in between. Every part of the rainforest depends on every other part.

above the canopy

Here, there is sunshine, wind, rain and changing temperatures.

canopy – the green roof

The canopy is 30–45 metres above the forest floor. Leaves struggle to reach the sunlight.

understorey – the forest rooms

Inside the forest, the air is moist and cool. The temperature hardly changes. Plants that like shade grow well here.

forest floor

The forest floor is covered in fallen leaves. Seeds and seedlings wait for a chance to grow.

soil – foundations

The soil is filled with bacteria, roots, fungi and small creatures.

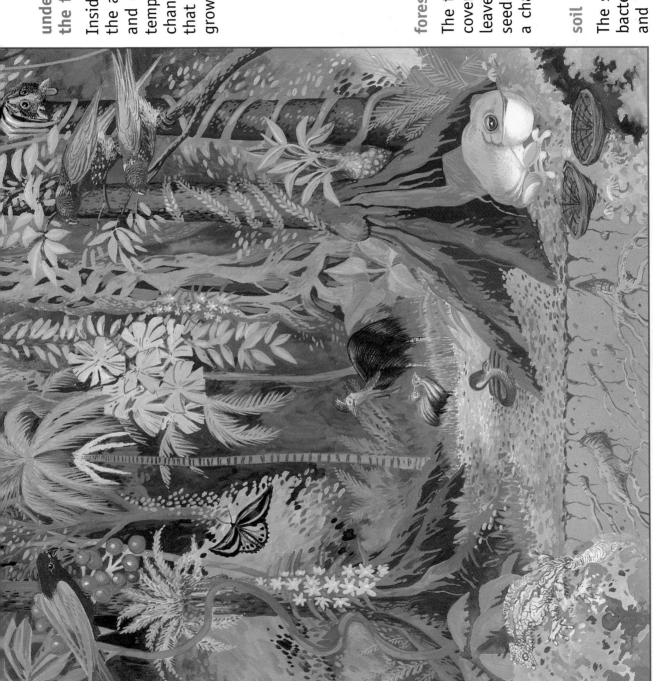

The forest floor

Inside the rainforest it is damp and cool. The light is dim. Leaves flutter down. Ripe fruit falls. Rotten branches, covered by green mosses and bright fungi, lie on the ground. Thick stems of vines snake across the forest floor.

A huge number of leaves, twigs, bits of wood and fruit fall onto the forest floor all through the year. This 'leaf litter' is quickly eaten by a huge number of animals which live on the forest floor. Beetles, ants, spiders and millipedes scurry amongst the leaf litter. Tiny animals munch the dead leaves. Beetles tunnel inside the wood. Fungi grow everywhere.

In the damp, warm rainforest, dead things rot and break down very fast. They go into the soil and become food for growing plants to use. Tropical rainforests are very good at feeding themselves.

Many of the animals living in the rainforest feed on leaves, fungi, flowers and fruit, but some animals feed on other animals. The forest floor is busy with animals hunting for a meal.

Velvet worms

The velvet worm walks through the leaf litter on fifteen pairs of fat purple legs, shooting jets of white, sticky slime out of its head at insects. The slime hardens around the insects like glue, and the velvet worm eats them.

Velvet worms are only 6 centimetres long. They are a very ancient group of animals.

Leeches

Little leeches loop along, searching for the fresh blood that is their food. They fasten onto the skin of birds, small animals and people, and begin sucking.

Rainforest plants

Each kind of rainforest plant grows in the best way it can to reach the sunlight.

Trees

Inside the forest, the trees grow straight and tall. Their leaves and branches are all far above, up in the sunlight. Rainforest trees do not waste energy growing branches low down. In the canopy, they push their neighbours out of the way to get more space.

Different kinds of trees grow next to each other in the rainforest. Some rainforest trees are a thousand years old.

15

Some rainforest trees grow flowers and fruit on their trunks, where they are easy to see. Birds, bats and possums eat the fruit and spread the seeds around the forest.

Most rainforest trees are evergreen. Some have pointed leaves with 'drip tips' to help rainwater run off quickly.

Huge roots, called 'buttress roots', spread out above the ground from some rainforest trees. The roots probably help to hold the trees firmly in the soil.

The strangler fig

A strangler fig gets to the sunlight by starting to grow in the top of a tree. Its roots grow down the trunk of the tree, feeling for the soil. Slowly, the roots of the strangler fig get thicker and join together around the trunk of the tree. Slowly, the tree dies. It rots, leaving the strangler fig growing around a hollow centre where the tree used to be.

Birds eat the fruit of the strangler fig and drop the seeds amongst the branches of other trees, high up in the canopy. Sometimes, a seed will sprout and a new strangler fig will start to grow.

Climbing plants

Climbing plants twist and loop through the rainforest. The climbing plants have their roots in the earth but use trees as climbing frames. Each plant is looking for the quickest way to get up to the sunlight.

Five ways of getting to the top

1 Twining

Twining vines wind round and round tree trunks on their way to the top. Sometimes, the trees die and rot away. Then the vines look like thick ropes, looping up to the canopy by themselves.

All twiners in the world twist the same way.

2. Scrambling

Scrambling plants have hooks, which fasten onto whatever they can reach. As the plant grows higher, it sends out more hooks.

The 'wait-a-while' is a climbing palm that grows in thick tangles, wherever it can find space and light. It has sharp hooks, which catch onto anything and everything.

3. Winding

Some vines have thin tendrils, like wires. As soon as the tendrils find something to hold on to, they wind tightly around it.

19

4 Leaning

Some kinds of vines just lean on a tree and grow upwards. Once in the sunshine, the vines grow leaves.

Sometimes, a vine will get too heavy and crash down. The vine does not break. It starts growing upwards again, leaning on another tree.

5 Gripping

Some vines have roots which grip onto the bark of tree trunks.

The ant plant

The rainforest is full of plants and animals that need each other and help each other.

The ant plant has tunnels in its bulging stems, which are just right for ants to live in. The ants put their droppings and bits of dead insects inside some of the tunnels. The ant plant uses this 'ant rubbish' for food.

A caterpillar lives inside the ant plant, and eats its leaves at night. The caterpillar is looked after by the ants. In return, the caterpillar makes a special honey mixture which the ants eat. The caterpillar, the ants and the ant plant all help each other and need each other. They all use the tree that the ant plant is living on.

Epiphytes

Some ferns grow on the forest floor. But in the rainforest, many ferns grow higher up on the trunks and branches of trees, closer to the light.

Ants, snails, spiders and frogs live in the ferns.

22

The ferns use the trees as walls and shelves to grow on. They do not harm the trees. The ferns feed on rainwater and on the leaves which fall into them and rot.

Plants that grow on other plants are called 'epiphytes'. Epiphytes have thousands of tiny seeds, which blow in the wind. Some seeds land in places where they can start to grow.

Staghorn ferns hang on to the tree by using a special kind of leaf.

The leaves of bird's nest ferns form a funnel to trap food.

Most rainforest orchids are epiphytes. So are mosses and lichens.

Basket ferns sometimes grow all the way around a branch or tree trunk.

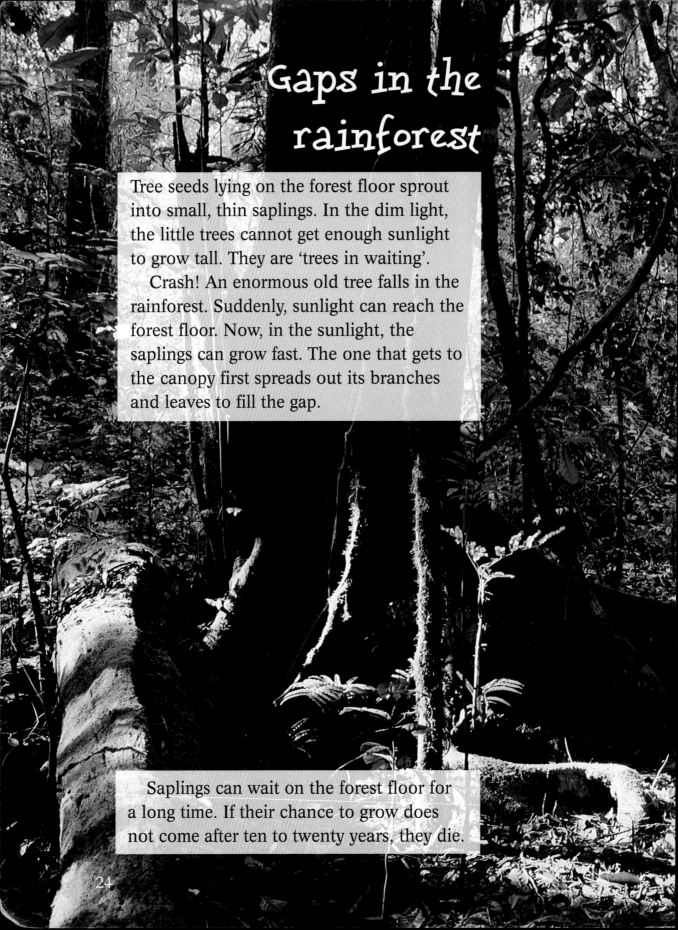

Gaps in the rainforest

Tree seeds lying on the forest floor sprout into small, thin saplings. In the dim light, the little trees cannot get enough sunlight to grow tall. They are 'trees in waiting'.

Crash! An enormous old tree falls in the rainforest. Suddenly, sunlight can reach the forest floor. Now, in the sunlight, the saplings can grow fast. The one that gets to the canopy first spreads out its branches and leaves to fill the gap.

Saplings can wait on the forest floor for a long time. If their chance to grow does not come after ten to twenty years, they die.

Stingers

The stinging shrub has pretty, heart-shaped leaves. Stingers grow in gaps in the forest, and along streams and paths. The leaves and stems are covered in tiny hairs with poisonous tips. The hairs are like splinters of glass.

Do not touch! If you do, the hairs stick in your skin and hurt for months.

In a rainforest, plants die and new plants grow all the time. Once a rainforest is growing strongly, it looks after itself. But if a rainforest is badly damaged, it takes hundreds of years for the rainforest to repair itself.

Gaps in the forest happen when

- ☀ branches fall off a tree
- ☀ storms blow trees over
- ☀ landslides or floods wash the soil away
- ☀ people cut down trees for timber
- ☀ a part of the forest is cleared to make fields, roads and houses

Small gaps happen all the time. Huge gaps change the forest, sometimes forever.

The rainforest in the day

As the sun rises, the rainforest is noisy with birds singing. Birds eat the fruit and flowers of the canopy. They flit between the tree trunks and scratch for insects on the forest floor.

Different animals feed on different plants in the rainforest at different times, so there is room for all. During the day, in the heat, many animals sleep and the forest is quiet.

Leaf-tailed gecko

The leaf-tailed gecko looks just like tree bark. When a predator comes near, the gecko waves its fat tail. It can let its tail drop off if the predator grabs it. The tail will keep on wriggling while the gecko escapes. Then the gecko grows another tail.

Python

A 7-metre-long python lies curled around a tree trunk. The python coils its body around its prey, squeezing it to death. One rat is enough food to last a python for three weeks.

The rainforest at night

At night, the rainforest is full of the sounds of animals – squeaks and grunts, scratchings and rustlings.

Small bats hunt insects. Rats and bandicoots scurry through the leaf litter. Giant spider webs hang between trees to catch moths and insects. Frogs croak by streams. Lizards wait for beetles. Owls hunt small animals. Possums climb among the branches, munching leaves.

Green ringtail possum

Not many animals want to eat stinger leaves or tough, poisonous fig leaves. But green ringtail possums can eat these leaves without being poisoned.

When morning comes, the green ringtail possum curls up in a tight ball in a nearby tree. The green colour of its fur helps to camouflage it.

Flying-foxes

Flying-foxes are huge bats. Their favourite food is the pollen and nectar of forest tree flowers. As night begins, thousands of flying-foxes fly in search of trees which have flowers. Pollen sticks to their fur, and they spread the pollen as they move from tree to tree.

Flying-foxes also eat fruit, dropping the seeds of the fruit as they fly.

Flying-foxes need rainforests for their food. But rainforests also need flying-foxes, because flying-foxes help to spread the seeds of rainforest plants.

Saving the rainforest

Tropical rainforests cover only a tiny part of Australia, yet they are home to more than half of all Australian plant and animal life. New things are being discovered about the rainforests all the time.

Many plants and animals that live in the rainforest depend on each other. The rainforest protects these special plants and animals. It is the only place where some of them live.

Rainforests seem to be very strong. In fact, they are very fragile because every part of the rainforest depends on every other part. If one part is destroyed then the whole rainforest is damaged.

Most of Australia's tropical rainforests are World Heritage Sites, which means that they are specially protected.

Index